ENGLAND
of One Hundred Years Ago
PHOTOGRAPH
COLLECTION

EAST SUSSEX

SELECTED BY AYLWIN GUILMANT

ALAN SUTTON

First published in the United Kingdom in 1992
by Alan Sutton Publishing Limited
Phoenix Mill, Stroud, Gloucestershire

First published in the United States of America
by Alan Sutton Publishing Incorporated
83 Washington Avenue, Dover, New Hampshire

British Library and Library of Congress
Cataloguing in Publication Data applied for

ISBN 0-7509-0306-6

Typesetting and origination by
Alan Sutton Publishing Limited
Graphics and Design Department.
Printed in Great Britain by
Bath Colour Books.

Some blemishes have been removed by extreme enlargement of the image to individual pixel
level, with careful computer graphics surgery to mend scratches, foxing, or other damage to the
photographic image.

ENGLAND
of One Hundred Years Ago
VOLUME NINE

East Sussex

The photograph collection of England of One Hundred Years Ago is an attempt to find and produce some of the best images in existence from late Victorian times up to the onset of the First World War. The country has been split into the traditional counties and this volume, numbered 9, represents East Sussex.

The criteria for selection are quality and clarity in the image together with subject interest. An attempt has been made to ensure a reasonable geographical balance within the area covered, but it has to be admitted that some areas were much more photographed than others.

The printed images are intended to be used for framing, although some people may wish to buy additional separate prints for framing by using the order form at the back of the book, and to keep this book intact. If the order form becomes separated from the book please write to the Phoenix Mill address advising the volume number and plate number you require.

The reproductions in this book are obtained by digital scanning and computer enhancement. Some blemishes have been removed by extreme enlargement of the image to individual pixel level, with careful computer graphics surgery to mend scratches, foxing, or other damage to the photographic image. The pictures on the facing page show a scratch, enlarged and repaired. Some damage, or blemishes in an otherwise interesting photograph are beyond reasonable repair, and have been left.

The monochrome image is then further enhanced by being artificially separated and printed in a four colour process with a sepia bias. The result is a high quality image with visual depth. The finished printed image is then protected by a careful application of matt varnish to reduce fading and to add protection. The paper is a super-calendared, acid free, matt art of 170 grammes weight per square metre.

The contents of the photographs remain totally genuine and the enhancement and surgery are used only to mend damage and not to create artificial images!

East Sussex at the end of the nineteenth century was still very much a rural area with many of the population employed either on the land or in fishing. These photographs, mainly the work of one photographer, George Woods, portray a peaceful time with rural activities and rustic characters, admittedly sometimes posed in romantic settings, but of a world long since passed.

George Woods (G.W. on the captions) was born in 1852 and worked as a draper and grocer in Wokingham for a number of years. After moving to Hastings he took up photography and until his death in 1934 took a large number of photographs of the east of the county. Most of these excellent photographs were donated by his family to Hastings Museum. A contemporary of Woods was Edward Reeves (E.R. in the captions) of Lewes, also a prolific photographer, whose collection of photographs is now preserved by the Sussex Archaeological Society.

Contents

Acknowledgements
We should like to thank the following for giving permission to reproduce their photographs: East Sussex Record Office, Hastings Museum, Sussex Archaeological Society, Towner Art Gallery and Museum, Eastbourne.

Plate 1. SUSSEX WOODMAN
Coppicing Woodland (G.W.)

Plate 2. CONTEMPLATION
Powdermill Pond near Battle (G.W.)

Plate 3. HASTINGS FISHERMEN
Preparing longlines (G.W.)

Plate 4. MEET US BY THE CROSS
The market cross at Alfriston (G.W.)

Plate 5. THE SHEPHERD
Guestling Church (G.W.)

Plate 6. CHATTING BY THE GATE
Farm near Ashburnham (G.W.)

Plate 7. THE GARDENER'S BROOM
Farm near Ashburnham (G.W.)

Plate 8. PLAYING IN THE WATER
Strand Quay, Rye (G.W.)

Plate 9. THE GAMEKEEPERS
(G.W.)

Plate 10. WASTE NOT: WANT NOT
East Well, Hastings (G.W.)

Plate 11. WHICH WAY?
Signpost at Winchelsea (G.W.)

Plate 12. KEEPER OF THE CASTLE
Herstmonceux Castle (G.W.)

Plate 13. THE GIANT SUNFLOWER
(G.W.)

Plate 14. THE STOCKS
Ninfield (G.W.)

Plate 15. THE FISHERMEN
Mill Bay, Robertsbridge (G.W.)

Plate 16. POTTING GERANIUMS
(G.W.)

Plate17. STACKING CORN
(G.W.)

Plate 18. PUT OUT THE FLAGS
The Albert Memorial, Hastings, 1897 (G.W.)

Plate 19. THE SOWER
(G.W.)

Plate 20. SHELLING WHELKS
Hastings Beach (G.W.)

Plate 21. COLLECTING FLOWERS
(G.W.)

Plate 22. SWAPPING TALES
Fishermen at Hastings (G.W.)

Plate 23. THE FLOWER SELLERS
Breeds Place, Hastings

Plate 24. GATHERING WOOD
(G.W.)

Plate 25. THE SERVANTS
Glyndebourne Farm, *c.* 1880

Plate 26. PIDDINGHOE
Near Lewes (G.W.)

Plate 27. BRINGING THE BEER
The Rock Brewery van, Maderia Drive, Brighton *c.* 1905

Plate 28. HOP PICKERS
(G.W.)